VET TECH COLORING BOOK

THIS BOOK BELONGS TO:

DON'T F*CK
with me
I KNOW HOW TO
CASTRATE

Sometimes
I MEET PEOPLE
AND
feel bad for their
DOG

Keep
Calm
you will finish
Vet Tech
School

VET TECH
Be nice or I'll
muzzle You.

i am a
VET TECH
whats your
SUPER POWER

I'm a
VET TECH
I can't fix
CRAZY
But i can
SEDATE IT

VETERINARY MEDICINE:
because people are gross.

VET TECHS
HAVE RHE BEST
PATIENTS

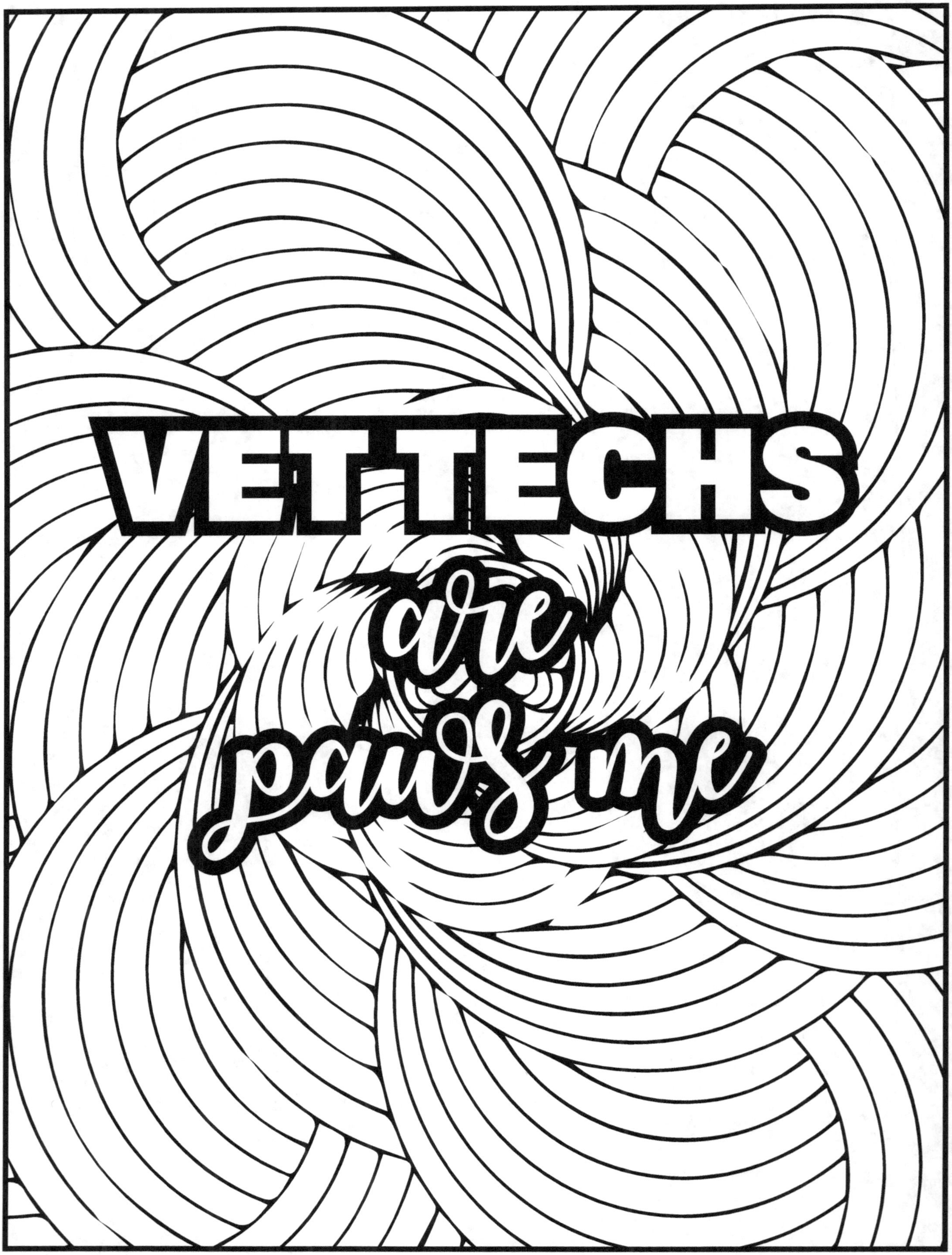
VET TECHS
are
paws me

VET TECH
NOT JUST
A JOB
it's
LOVE

REAL MEN
MARRY
VET TECHS

49% Vet Tech
51% Sexy Beast

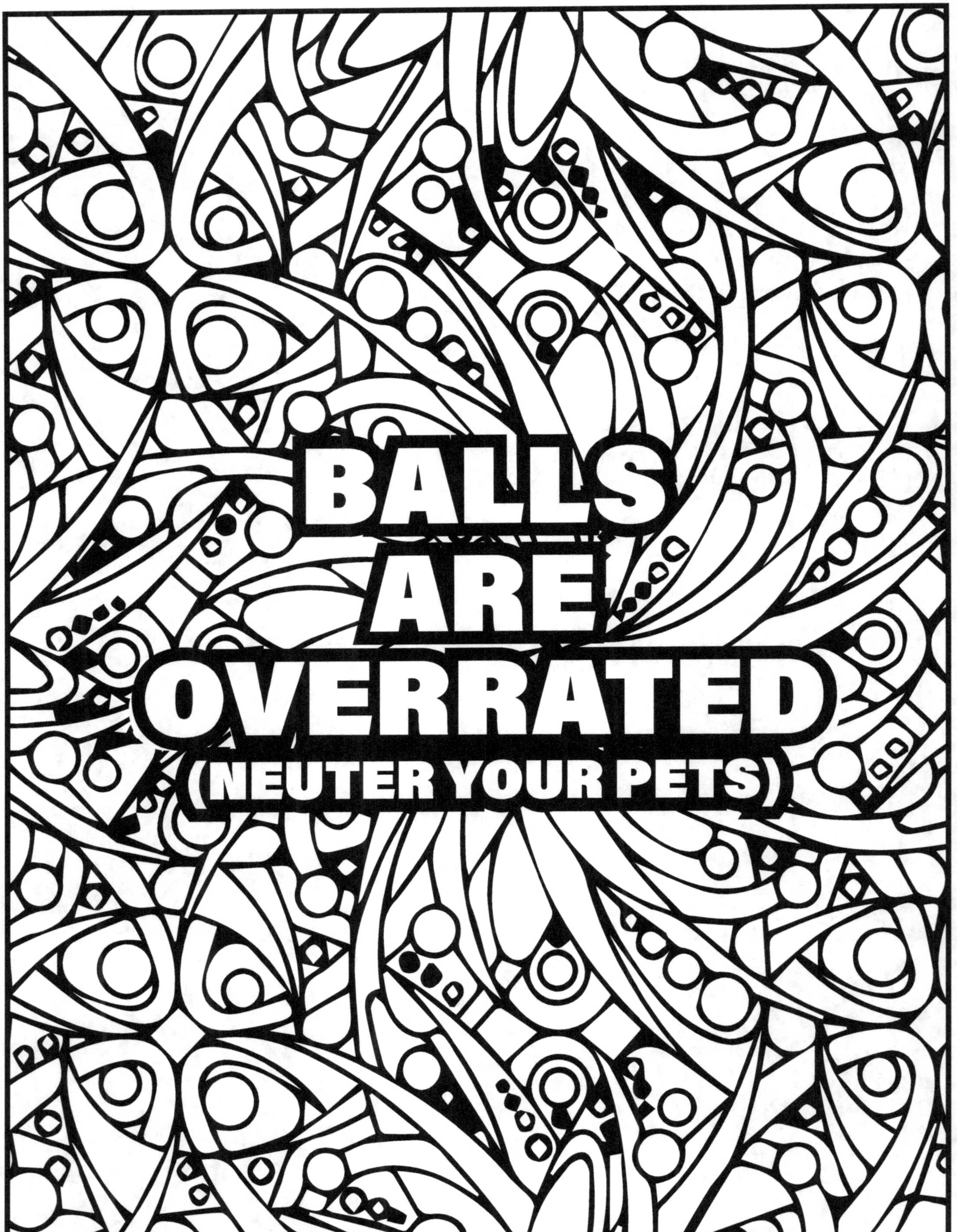
BALLS
ARE
OVERRATED
(NEUTER YOUR PETS)

Don't
make me
use My
Vet Tech
Voice

COOLEST
Vet
Tech
Ever

BEST
vet tech
EVER

WAKE UP
DRINK COFFEE
SAVE
ANIMALS

BITE ME
I'M A
VET TECH

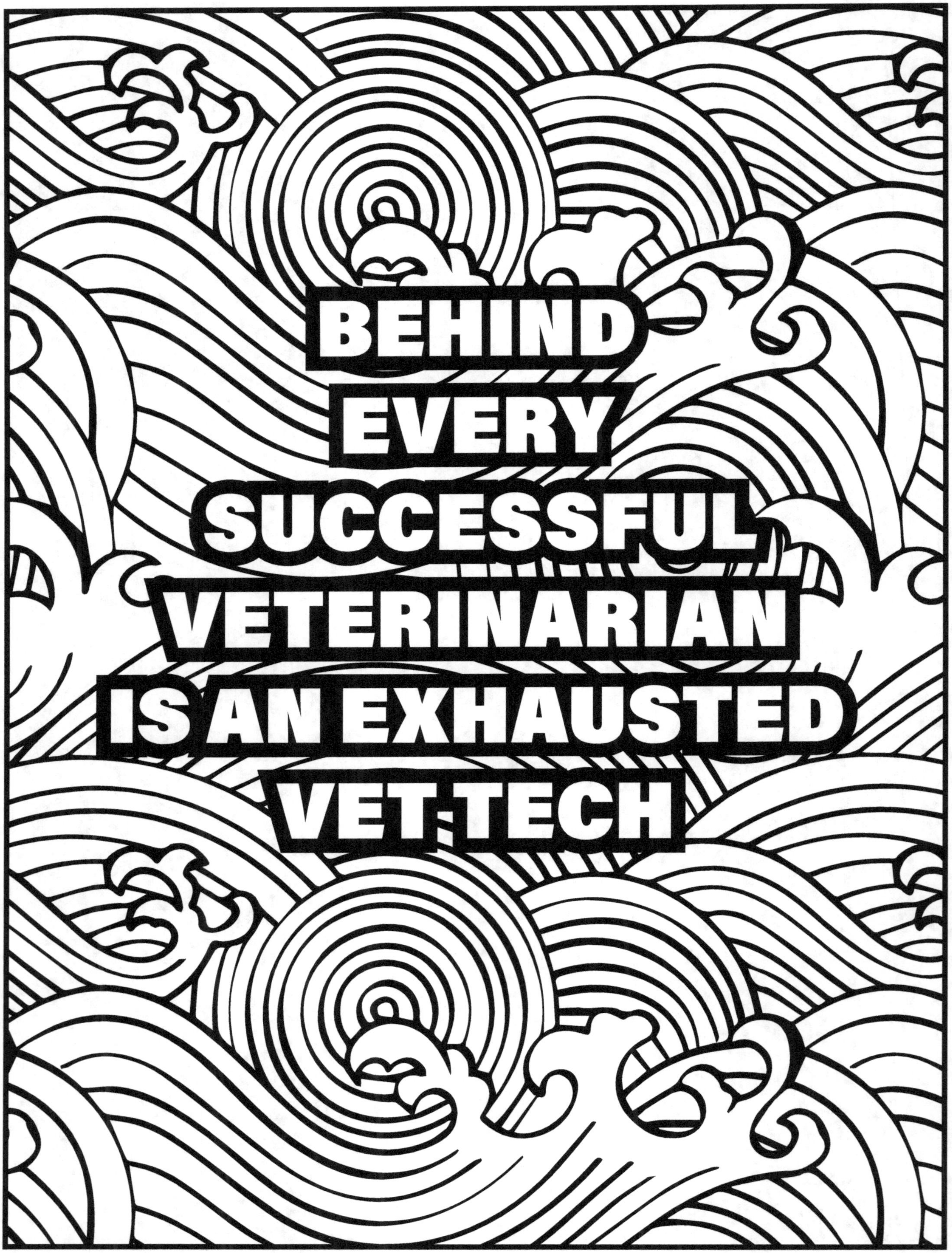
BEHIND
EVERY
SUCCESSFUL
VETERINARIAN
IS AN EXHAUSTED
VET TECH

THIS
Vet Tech
NEEDS A
Cat Nap

I WAS MADE TO
SAVE
ANIMALS

VET TECHS
are
AWESOME

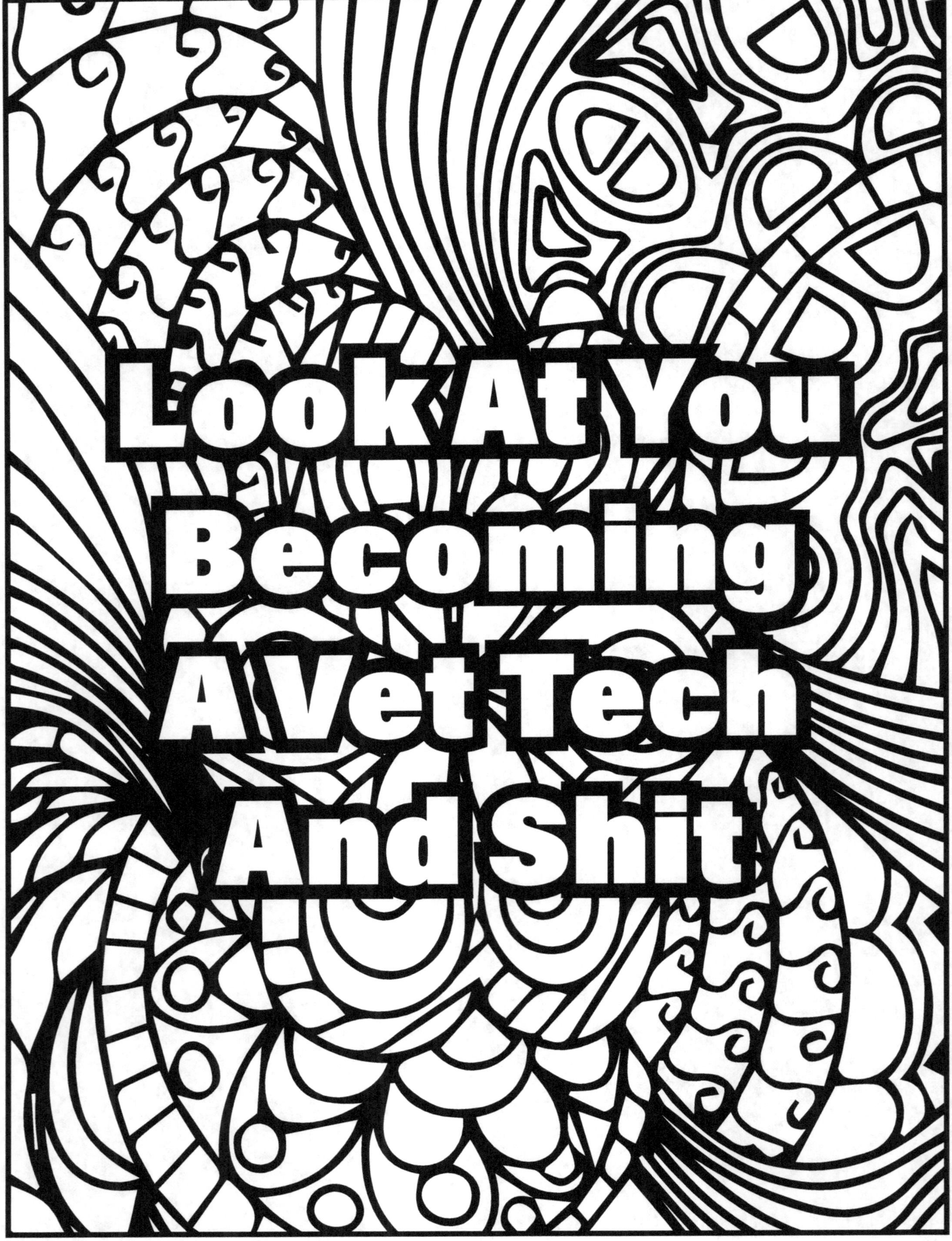
Look At You
Becoming
A Vet Tech
And Shit

Freaking
Amazing
Veterinary
Receptionist

I became a
VET
TECH

I'm a
VET TECH
because
ANIMALS
need superheroes too!

SAID NO
Vet Tech
EVER

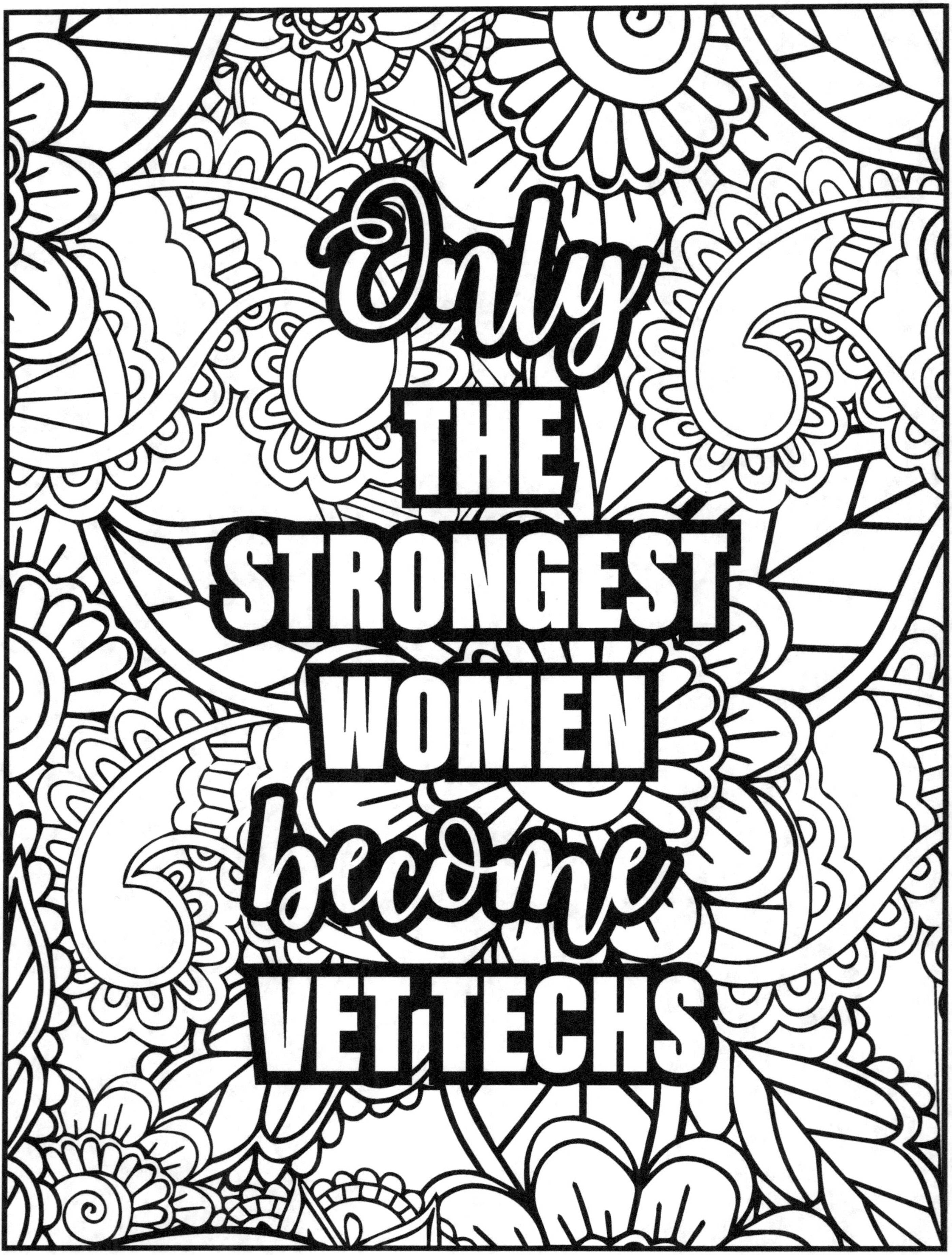
Only
THE
STRONGEST
WOMEN
become
VET TECHS

VET
TECH
MAKE A
difference

GOD MADE
VET TECH
so animals can have
HEROES
TOO

www.ingramcontent.com/pod-product-compliance
Lightning Source LLC
Chambersburg PA
CBHW080623220526
45466CB00010B/3446
9798550079355